THIRD SYNOD OF METZ

THIRD SYNOD OF METZ

RATBOD OF METZ

Copyright 2025 by Dalcassian Press

All rights reserved. No part of this book may be reproduced in any manner whatsoever without written permission except in the case of brief quotations embodied in critical articles and reviews.

No part of this publication may be reproduced, distributed, or transmitted in any form or by any means, including photocopying, recording, or other electronic or mechanical methods, without the prior written permission of the publisher, except in the case of brief quotations embodied in critical reviews and certain other non-commercial uses permitted by copyright law. For permission requests, write to Dalcassian Press at admin@thescriptoriumproject.com

Translator: Curtin, D.P. (1985-)

ISBN: 979-8-3492-6918-9 (Paperback)
ISBN: 979-8-3492-6919-6 (eBook)
Library of Congress Control Number:

Printed by Ingram Content Group, 1 Ingram Blvd, La Vergne, Tennessee
First Printing 2025, Dalcassian Press, Wilmington, DE

This work is part of a series produced in association with the Scriptorium Project and its community of scholars and translators.
Please visit our website at: www.thescriptoriumproject.com

LATIN TEXT

Anno ab incarnatione domini nostri Iesu Christi DCCCXCIII, regni domini Arnulfi gloriosissimi regis, die Calendarum Maiarum, acta est synodus in suburbio Metensis civitatis, in ecclesia Sancti Arnulfi, ab archiepiscopo venerabili Ratbodo Treverensi, et a Rotberto prædictæ civitatis præsule. Dado quoque Virdunensis ecclesiæ reverendissimus episcopus et Arnoldus Tullensium episcopus et Stephanus inclytus abbas et multi sacerdotes cum comitibus et pluribus nobilibus et deum timentibus viris adfuerunt. Ubi pari voto, parique consensu, pro vera caritate et tranquillitate sanctæ dei ecclesiæ, quam redemit Christus sanguine suo, sibi invicem occurentes, hæc in commune præsules locuti sunt.

Cap. I. Quod pax a paganis et contumacibus christianis per emendationem morum a deo impetranda sit.

Episcopi et presbyteri et fideles laici, qui ante nos fuerunt, iuxta sacram canonum auctoritatem, sæpius in Christi nomine convenientes, iustitiam dei statuerunt et idcirco pacem suis diebus habuerunt iuxta illud, quod scriptum est: Pax multa diligentibus legem tuam, domine. Et, hominibus bonæ voluntatis. Nos autem, qui tanto tempore transacto comprovincialem synodum non habuimus, et invicem quærere misericordiam dei neglexeximus, videmus in nobis completum esse, quod per prophetam dominus dicit: Terram vestram in conspectu vestro alieni devorant, et erit in vastitate hostili. Ergo qualiter a Nortmannis hæc omnia in nobis completa sint, nemo dubitat, quomodo etiam a perversis christianis undique atteramur, omnes in commune sentimus, sicut scriptum est: Populum tuum, domine, humiliaverunt et hæreditatem tuam vexaverunt. Quærenda est igitur pietas Christi, qua pagani arceantur, et statuenda est lex dei, qua crudelissimi nostræ gentis homines a vastatione pauperum repellantur. Idcirco, quicquid in nobis pravæ voluntatis est, abiciamus et de paganis Christo auxiliante pacem obtinere valebimus. Auctoritatem sanctorum patrum contumacibus nostris imponamus, et velint nolint, pro timore etiam gloriosissimi nostri senioris Arnulfi regis, ad satisfactionem venire faciemus, et sic iustitiam dei statuendo, poterimus eius misericordiam invenire, quem nos cognoscimus pravis actibus graviter offendisse.

Cap. II. Ut decimas ecclesiæ solus sacerdos accipiat; nullam illarum partem laici seniores usurpent.

Dominus loquitur per prophetam dicens: Adferte omnem decimam in horreis meis et probate me in hoc, dicit dominus, si non aperuero vobis cataractas cæli, et dedero vobis fructus usque ad abundantiam. Scimus enim, quoniam peccatis exigentibus clauditur cælum, et fit nostris diebus sæpissime fames. Ideo statuimus, ut deinceps nemo seniorum de ecclesia sua accipiat de decimis aliquam portionem, sed solummodo sacerdos, qui eo loco servit, ubi antiquitus decimæ fuerant consecratæ, ipse eas cum integritate accipiat in sui sustentationem et ad luminaria concinnanda et basilicæ ædificia, vestimenta quoque sacerdotalia et cætera utensilia suo ministerio congrua obtinenda. Hæc omnia episcopi de suis ecclesiis, et cæteri attendere decreverunt.

Cap. III. Ut unus presbyter unam solummodo habeat ecclesiam.

Unusquisque presbyter unam solummodo habeat ecclesiam, nisi forte antiquitus habuerit capellam vel membrum aliquod adiacens sibi, quod non expedit separari. Est enim multum laudabile coram deo et hominibus, si unus presbyter unam ecclesiam salubriter providerit et utiliter rexerit. Quoniam non est nobis cura animarum adhibenda pro temporali commoditate, sed cunctis sacerdotibus est optandum, ut cum suis ovibus a Christo recipiant pascua vitæ æternæ.

Cap. IV. Ut de manso ecclesiæ nullus census exigatur et ne pro sepultura pretium detur.

De uno manso et de terris pro sepultura datis, et pro quatuor mancipiis vel eorum procreatione nullus census deinceps exigatur; et pro sepultura nullum pretium detur.

Cap. V. Ut nullam in domo sua feminam habeant sacerdotes.

Sacerdotes, qui vice Mosis iram domini super populum sævientem precibus suis debent mitigare, attendentes etiam, ne illud fiat, quod scriptum est, maxima ruina populi in culpa sacerdotum fuit, nequaquam in sua domo secum aliquam feminam habeant, nec matrem, nec sororem, sed auferentes omnem occasionem satanæ, angelicam vitam ducant et domino deo casto corpore et mundo corde finetenus serviant. Nam licet hoc in sacris litteris crebrius inhibitum esse videatur, tamen quia hoc nefas in quibusdam oriri videbatur, idcirco communi decreto statutum est, et hoc interdictum a sancta synodo nimium laudatum est.

Cap VI. Ut presbyteri libros et vestimenta sacerdotalia ostendant episcopo et chrisma sub sera custodiant; clerici armis aut laicorum indumentis ne utantur, et de iis qui infantes in baptismo suscipiunt.

Cuncti presbyteri ut libros et sacerdotalia vestimenta suo episcopo in proxima synodo ostendant, et ut chrisma suum sub sigillo et sera semper custodiant, a prædictis episcopis expresse commendatum est. Et ut nemo clericorum arma portet vel indumenta laicalia induat, id est, cottos vel mantellos sine cappa non portet, et laici cappas non portent. Et nullus alteri suscipiat a fonte infantem, nisi qui apprime signaculum, id est abrenunciationem diaboli et professionem catholicæ fidei tenuerit. Et infantem nequaquam duo vel plures, sed unus a fonte baptismatis suscipiat, quia in huiuscemodi secta diabolo datur locus, et tanti ministerii reverentia vilescit. Nam unus deus, unum baptisma, unus, qui a fonte suscipit, debet esse pater vel mater infantis. Hæc omnia generaliter interdicta sunt, quia et grandis levitas erat, et gravitas vel religio clericalis nimis in talibus vilis efficiebatur.

Cap. VI. Ut nemo cum Iudeis edat aut bibat.
Guntbertus Metensis ecclesiæ primicerius obtulit libellum proclamationis super Iudæos, qui habitant Metis. Quapropter interdictum est, iuxta capitula sanctorum patrum, ut nemo christianorum cum eis manducet et bibat, vel quicquid comedi aut potari potest, a Iudæis accipiat. Nimis enim, iuxta quod ait Cæsarius Arelatensis ecclesiæ episcopus, indignum est atque sacrilegum, eorum cibos a christianis sumi, cum ea, quibus nos fruimur, ab illis iudicentur immunda, ac sic inferiores incipiant esse christiani quam Iudæi. Et omnes eorum convivas ipse et sanctus Siagrius Eduorum episcopus cum aliis multis excommunicaverunt.

Cap. VII. De his, qui putabant pro defendendis ecclesiasticis rebus licere excommunicatis communicare. (De his, qui putabant pro defendendis ecclesiæ rebus licere communicare excommunicatis.)
Placuit sanctæ synodo, hunc errorem quasi pium ab æcclesia amovere, quia animarum curam a domino accepimus, non pecuniarum. Inde et reddituri sumus deo rationem et accepturi propter suam misericordiam æternam retributionem vel iustam damnationem.

Cap. VIII. Ut missæ in locis non consecratis non fiant; et basilicæ a chorepiscopis consecratæ ab episcopis consecrentur.
In locis vero non consecratis, id est in solariis sive in cubiculis, propter infirmos, vel longius iter, a quibusdam presbyteris sacrificium offerebatur, quod omnimodis interdictum est. Et ut basilicæ a chorepiscopis consecratæ ab episcopis consecrentur, roboratum est, quia iuxta decreta Damasi papæ, Innocentii et Leonis vacuum est atque inane, quicquid in summi sacerdotii chorepiscopi egerunt ministerio; et quod et ipsi iidem sint qui et presbyteri, sufficienter invenitur.

Cap. IX. De duabus sanctimonialibus ob facinus in ergastulum retrusis, et de diacono sacrilegium confesso.

Duæ sanctimoniales propter suum facinus de monasterio sancti Petri sine velamine erant eiectæ, sed iuxta sacros canones sancta constituit synodus, ut velamina illis redderentur et intra monasterium in ergastulo ponerentur, parvo pane et aqua brevi, cum abundantia divini verbi usque ad satisfactionem fruerentur. Quidam etiam diaconus, qui de sacrilegio confessus et convictus fuit, pro misericordia in carcere poni iussus est, interdicto ministerio, et ut pro eo omnes generaliter orarent, iniunctum est.

Cap. X. Excommunicati qui Folcardum presbyterum evirarant.

Quædam femina, nomine Ava, cum sui fratris consilio et auxilio, qui vocatur Folcrius, et cum aliis consanguineis suis, suum maritum dimisit et ad eum redire noluit. Unde illorum sacerdos servus dei, vocabulo Folcardus, ad suam dominam et ad eius fratrem veniens, ut eos a tanto scelere traheret, confestim ab eodem et suis complicibus castratus est. Pro his omnibus ad synodum vocati venire noluerunt, et idcirco usque ad satisfactionem excommunicati sunt.

Cap. XI. Excommunicati provinciæ vastatores, item Theodricus et Lantbertus.

Viri pestilentes vastabant miserabiliter istam provinciam. Pro quo scelere ad synodum vocati, sicut scriptum est: Eripite pauperem et egenum, alii venerunt, alii venire noluerunt. Illi qui adfuerunt, synodo satisfecerunt; cæteri autem canonice excommunicati sunt. Pari etiam tenore excommunicatus est quidam homo, vocabulo Theodricus, cum complicibus suis, quia quandam viduam fugiendo prostratam super corpus sancti Eventii rapuit et de monasterio traxit, et in uxorem sibi eam taliter sociavit. Quidam vir nomine Lantbertus interficiens consanguineum suum, et ducens eius uxorem nomine Vualdradam, iuravit coram archiepiscopo, quod tale coniugium dimitteret, et iterum ei se sociavit et adhuc eam habet; idcirco excommunicatus est.

Cap. XII. Excommunicati, qui communionem habebant cum excommunicatis.

Quæsitum est a sancta synodo, quid de iis sacra fieri auctoritas iuberet, qui cum prædictis excommunicatis communionem habeant. Nam non tantum laici, verum etiam presbyteri in celebratione missæ excommunicatos recipiunt; et quid de his, qui in eadem excommunicatione mortui fuerint. Verum ad hæc tanta auctoritas prolata est. Sanctus Petrus apostolus in ordinatione sancti Clementis ita plebes alloquitur: Si inimicus est alicui pro actibus suis, vos cum illo nolite amici esse; et prudenter observare debetis, avertere vos ab eo, cui ipsum sentitis adversum, sed nec loqui his, quibus ipse non loquitur. Istius transgressores sanctus Petrus et omnis auctoritas excommunicat. Servis autem ac propriis libertis sive beneficiatis, venerabiles episcopi in communione dominorum absolutionem dederunt. Sanctus Leo papa de excommunicatis et ita defunctis taliter decrevit: Horum causa iudicio dei est servanda, in cuius manu fuit, ut talium obitus usque ad communionis remedium differetur. Nos autem, quibus viventibus non communicavimus, mortuis communicare non possumus.

Cap. XIII. Preces cum triduano ieiunio indictæ pro rege.

Precando rogaverunt prædicti episcopi, orare pro domino rege Arnulfo, et triduanum in proximo celebrare ieiunium, ubi cum litaniis et magna corporis adflictione precaremur deum, ut faciat nos converti ad se in toto corde et animo volenti, adaperiat cor nostrum in lege sua et in præceptis suis, et faciat pacem, et placeat redemptori nostro eripere oppressos, revocare in angustiis constitutos. Et sic talia agendo mereamur obtinere hic indulgentiam et in futuro pacem sine fine mansuram.

Amen.

CONCILIUM METENSE

Epistola synodalis episcoporum regni Lotharii ad Hincmarum Remensem:

Optabili in Christo fratri Igmaro Theodgaudus primas Belgicæ Galliæ, Guntharius Agrippinensis Coloniæ et Arduicus Vosotiocensis ecclesiæ episcopi eorumque cœpiscopi salutem et pacem.

Relegimus, frater et utinam frater Igmare, libellum tuæ accusationis adversus Hilduinum dilectum filium et fratrem nostrum, ut credimus, idoneum virum, in quo ipsum officio pastorali indignum asseveras, et causas te scire, pro quibus isdem electus ordinari non debeat, exclamas. Quamvis ab hac improbitate hoc solummodo te revocare vel temperare debuisset, quod ille tuus domnus et nutritor fuerit carus, si tamen memor et non ingratus fore voluisses, cuius iste et affinitatem refert et nomen. Nunc quoniam delator esse delegisti, quod restat non omittas. Te enim expoliasti iudicio, dum criminationis cartulam, quod tuo officio et honori, ut æstimamus, non competebat, propria manu, quod negare non potes, in conventu regum principi nostro Hlothario inconsulte porrexisti ac memoratum Hildiwinum nosque pariter suspectos reddidisti. Ergo quia te obiecta probaturum promisisti, consequens est, ut exequaris quæ proposuisti; unde et te canonica commonemus auctoritate, ut accusationis tuæ executionem canonice prosequaris. Quod si te accusationi subtraxeris et probationi defueris, noveris te canonicis de accusatoribus regulis subiacere. Calumniæ vero, quas synodalibus decretis obumbrare nisus es, in te atque in æquivocum nepotem tuum, qui ita provecti estis, reflectuntur. Quorum neuter ex illa fuit ecclesia, in qua ambitione atque favore potentatus inthronizatus esse dinoscitur. Hac conditione dehinc exigente synodo te adesse oportebit, quæ Idus Martias apud urbem Mediomatricum, Christi favente gratia, celebrabitur. Ubi sæpefatus frater aut tua probatione convincatur aut sua defensione liberetur. Ubi quoque et nos tibi ex omnibus, quæ de ecclesia Camaracensi scribens monuisti et reprehendisti, rationes reddendo respondere valeamus.

In Christo te valere optamus.

THIRD SYNOD OF METZ

In the year from the incarnation of our Lord Jesus Christ 893, in the reign of the most glorious Lord King Arnulf, on the day of the Kalends of May, a synod was held in the suburb of the city of Metz, in the church of Saint Arnulf, by the venerable Archbishop Ratbod of Treves, and by Robert, the bishop of the aforementioned city. Also present were the most reverend bishop of the church of Verdun, Dado, and Arnold, the bishop of Toul, and the illustrious abbot Stephen, and many priests with counts and numerous noble and God-fearing men. There, with equal desire and consent, for the true love and tranquility of the holy Church of God, which Christ redeemed with His blood, the prelates spoke together.

Chapter I. *That peace from pagans and obstinate Christians should be sought from God through the amendment of morals.*
Bishops, priests, and faithful laymen who have been before us, according to the sacred authority of the canons, frequently convening in the name of Christ, established the justice of God and therefore had peace in their days according to that which is written: "Great peace have they who love Your law, O Lord." And, "To men of goodwill." But we, who have not had a provincial synod for such a long time, and have neglected to seek God's mercy from one another, see in ourselves what the prophet says is fulfilled: "Aliens devour your land in your presence, and it will be in a hostile desolation." Therefore, no one doubts how all these things have been fulfilled in us by the Northmen, how we are also oppressed on all sides by perverse Christians; we all feel together, as it is written: "Your people, O Lord, they have humbled, and your inheritance they have vexed." Therefore, the piety of Christ must be sought, by which pagans may be repelled, and the law of God must be

established, by which the cruelest of our people may be turned away from the devastation of the poor. Therefore, let us cast away whatever is of wicked will in us, and with Christ's help, we will be able to obtain peace from the pagans. Let us impose the authority of the holy fathers on our obstinate ones, and whether they will or not, out of fear of our most glorious elder King Arnulf, we will make them come to satisfaction, and thus by establishing the justice of God, we will be able to find His mercy, whom we know we have grievously offended by wicked deeds.

Chapter II. *That only the priest should receive the tithes of the church; let no part of them be usurped by lay elders.*
The Lord speaks through the prophet saying: "Bring all the tithes into my storehouse and test me in this, says the Lord, if I will not open the windows of heaven for you and pour out for you a blessing until there is no more need." For we know that heaven is closed due to the demands of sins, and famine occurs very frequently in our days. Therefore, we decree that henceforth no elder of the church shall receive any portion of the tithes, but only the priest who serves in the place where the tithes were consecrated in ancient times, he shall receive them with integrity for his sustenance and for preparing the lights and building the basilica, as well as for obtaining priestly garments and other utensils suitable for his ministry. All these things the bishops have decreed to observe from their churches.

Chapter III. *That each priest should have only one church.*
Let each priest have only one church, unless he has had an ancient chapel or some adjacent member that is not expedient to separate. For it is very commendable before God and men if one priest provides healthily for and governs one church usefully. For we should not care for souls for temporal advantage, but all priests should desire to receive pastures of eternal life with their sheep from Christ.

Chapter IV. *That no rent should be exacted from the manor of the church, nor should any price be given for burial.*
From one manor and from lands given for burial, and for four servile persons or their offspring, let no rent be exacted henceforth; and for burial, let no price be given.

Chapter V. *That priests should have no woman in their house.*
Priests, who should mitigate the Lord's anger over the raging people with their prayers, also considering that what is written—that the greatest ruin of the people was in the fault of the priests—should not have any woman with them in their house, neither mother nor sister, but removing every occasion of Satan, they should lead an angelic life and serve the Lord God with a chaste body and pure heart. For although this seems to be frequently prohibited in the sacred scriptures, nevertheless, because this wickedness seemed to arise in some cases, therefore it was established by common decree, and this prohibition was greatly commended by the holy synod.

Chapter VI. *That priests should show their books and priestly garments to the bishop and keep chrism under seal; clerics should not use weapons or lay garments, and regarding those who receive infants in baptism.*
All priests should show their books and priestly garments to their bishop at the next synod, and they should keep their chrism under seal and lock at all times, as expressly commended by the aforementioned bishops. And let no cleric bear arms or wear lay garments, that is, let him not wear tunics or mantles without a cape, and let laymen not wear capes. And let no one receive an infant from the font except for the one who holds the seal, that is, the renunciation of the devil and the profession of the Catholic faith. And let not two or more receive an infant, but one should receive from the font of baptism, because in such a sect there is room given to the devil, and the reverence of such a ministry is diminished. For there is one God, one baptism; the one

who receives from the font should be the father or mother of the infant.

All these things are generally forbidden, because there was great levity, and the gravity or religiousness of the clergy was made too cheap in such matters.

Chapter VI. *That no one eat or drink with the Jews. Guntbertus, the primicerius of the church of Metz, offered a proclamation concerning the Jews who dwell in Metz.*

Therefore, according to the decrees of the holy fathers, it is forbidden that any Christians eat or drink with them, or receive anything that can be eaten or drunk from the Jews. For, as Cæsarius, bishop of the church of Arles, said, it is unworthy and sacrilegious for Christians to take their food, since what we enjoy is judged by them to be unclean, and thus Christians begin to be inferior to the Jews. And both he and the holy Siagrius, bishop of the Eudores, excommunicated all their guests.

Chapter VII. *About those who thought it permissible to communicate with excommunicated persons for the defense of ecclesiastical matters.*

It pleased the holy synod to remove this error from the church as pious, because we have received the care of souls from the Lord, not of money. Hence, we shall also render an account to God and receive, for His eternal mercy, either just retribution or just condemnation.

Chapter VIII. *That Masses not be held in unconsecrated places; and that basilicas consecrated by chorepiscopi be consecrated by bishops.*

In unconsecrated places, that is, in solariums or in chambers, for the sick or for long journeys, sacrifices were offered by certain priests, which is altogether forbidden. And it was strengthened that basilicas consecrated by chorepiscopi be consecrated by bishops, because, according to the decrees of Pope Damasus, Innocent, and Leo, whatever was done in the ministry of the highest priesthood by chorepiscopi is void and empty; and it is sufficiently found that they themselves are the same as priests.

Chapter IX. *About two nuns imprisoned for a crime, and about a deacon who confessed sacrilege.*
Two nuns were expelled from the monastery of Saint Peter without veils because of their crime, but according to the sacred canons, the holy synod decreed that the veils be returned to them and that they be placed in the monastery in prison, with little bread and water briefly, while enjoying the abundance of the divine word until satisfaction. A certain deacon, who confessed and was convicted of sacrilege, was ordered to be placed in prison for mercy, under interdiction from ministry, and it was commanded that all should generally pray for him.

Chapter X. *Excommunicated are those who castrated the priest Folcard.*
A certain woman named Ava, with the counsel and assistance of her brother, who is called Folcrius, and with other relatives, left her husband and did not want to return to him. Therefore, their priest, a servant of God named Folcard, coming to his lady and her brother to draw them away from such a crime, was immediately castrated by the same and his accomplices. For all these things, they were summoned to the synod but did not want to come, and therefore they were excommunicated until satisfaction.

Chapter XI. *Excommunicated are the devastators of the province, also Theodric and Lantbert.*
Pestilent men were miserably ravaging this province. For this crime, they were summoned to the synod, as it is written: "Rescue the poor and needy," some came, others did not want to come. Those who were present satisfied the synod; however, the others were canonically excommunicated. In like manner, a certain man named Theodric was excommunicated with his accomplices because he, fleeing, seized a certain widow prostrated over the body of Saint Eventius and dragged her from the monastery, and thus joined her to himself as a wife. A

certain man named Lantbert, killing his relative and leading away his wife named Vualdrada, swore before the archbishop that he would dismiss such a marriage, and again joined himself to her and still has her; therefore, he was excommunicated.

Chapter XII. *Excommunicated are those who had communion with the excommunicated.*

The holy synod inquired what should be done regarding those who have communion with the aforementioned excommunicated. For not only laypeople but also priests receive excommunicated persons in the celebration of Mass; and what should be done about those who have died in the same excommunication. However, such authority was pronounced. Saint Peter the Apostle, in the ordination of Saint Clement, thus addresses the people: "If someone is an enemy to you because of their deeds, do not be friends with him; and you should prudently observe, turn away from him of whom you feel adversarial, and do not speak to those whom he does not speak to." Those who transgress this, Saint Peter and all authority excommunicate. However, for servants and their own freedmen or beneficiaries, venerable bishops granted absolution in communion with their lords. Pope Saint Leo decreed thus about the excommunicated and those who have died: "Their case is to be kept for the judgment of God, in whose hand it was, that the deaths of such may be deferred until the remedy of communion." But we, who did not communicate with the living, cannot communicate with the dead.

Chapter XIII. *Prayers with a three-day fast appointed for the king.*

The aforementioned bishops prayed, asking to pray for the Lord King Arnulf, and to celebrate a three-day fast in the near future, where, with litanies and great affliction of body, we would pray to God that He may cause us to turn to Him with all our heart and willing spirit, that He may open our heart in His law and in His commandments, and may grant peace, and may it please our Redeemer to rescue the oppressed, to recall those in distress. And thus, by doing such things, may we deserve to obtain here indulgence and in the future everlasting peace. Amen.

COUNCIL OF METZ
Letter from the bishops of the kingdom of Lothair to Hincmar of Reims

To our beloved brother Igmar, Theodgaudus, primate of Belgic Gaul, Guntharius of Cologne, and Arduicus of the Vosges, and their fellow bishops, greetings and peace.

We have read, brother, and may you be a brother, the document of your accusation against Hilduin, our beloved son and brother, whom we believe to be a suitable man, in which you assert that he is unworthy of the pastoral office, and you exclaim the reasons you know for which he should not be ordained. Although you should have been deterred or refrained from this wickedness solely because he has been dear to you as your lord and nurturer, if, however, you had wished to be mindful and not ungrateful, to whom he is related and whose name he bears. Now that you have chosen to be an accuser, do not omit what remains. For you have stripped yourself of judgment, as you presented the document of accusation, which we believe was not fitting for your office and honor, with your own hand, in the assembly of the kings to our prince Hlothar, and you made both Hilduin and us equally suspicious. Therefore, since you promised to prove the accusations, it follows that you must carry out what you proposed; hence we also remind you by canonical authority to pursue the execution of your accusation canonically. But if you withdraw from the accusation and fail to provide proof, know that you are subject to the canonical rules regarding accusers. The calumnies, which you attempted to obscure with synodal decrees, reflect upon you and upon your ambiguous grandson, who have advanced in such a manner. Neither of you belonged to that church, in which it is known that you were enthroned through ambition and the favor of the powerful. Under this condition, the synod will require you to be present, which will be celebrated on the Ides of March in the city of Médiomatricum, with the grace of Christ. Where your brother will either be convicted by your proof or be freed by his own defense. There, we will also be able to respond to you regarding all that you have written and criticized about the church of Camaracensis.

We wish you to be well in Christ.

This work was produced in association with:

www.ingramcontent.com/pod-product-compliance
Lightning Source LLC
LaVergne TN
LVHW061050070526
838201LV00074B/5244